LIGHT

BY

JOANNA BRUNDLE

©2017
Book Life
King's Lynn
Norfolk PE30 4LS

ISBN: 978-1-78637-209-3

Written by:
Joanna Brundle

Edited by:
Charlie Ogden

Designed by:
Drue Rintoul

Photocredits
Abbreviations: l-left, r-right, b-bottom, t-top, c-centre, m-middle.

Front Cover t – Alexandru Chiriac. Front Cover mt – J. Helgason. Front Cover mb – Muzhik. Front Cover b – Ng Wei Keong. 1 – jaboo2foto. 2 – Chones. 3t – rangizzz. 3b – photosync. 4t – Romolo Tavani. 4b – Everett Historical. 5t – Amanda Carden. 5b – Puwadol Jaturawutthichai. 6t – By Photograph by Oren Jack Turner, Princeton, N.J. (The Library of Congress) [Public domain], via Wikimedia Commons. 6b – PlanilAstro. 7t – phive. 7b – Dawid Lech. 8t – Carlos Horta. 8b – Johanna Altmann. 9t – majeczka. 10b – olavs. 11t – Evgeniya Anikienko. 11b – RTimages. 12t – MilanB. 12m – Evgheni Manciu. 12b – loskutnikov. 13t – MrIncredible. 13b – designelements. 14tr – Georgios Kollidas. 14ml – kasezo. 14b – PongMoji. 15t – Billion Photos. 15m – Ondrej Prosicky. 15b – Foto-Ruhrgebiet. 17m – Biehler Michael. 17b – Michal Ninger. 18t – Djaile. 18b – Maciej Bledowski. 18inset – dreamerb. 20t – kavram. 20b – Pepe Baeza. 21t – CreativeHQ. 21b – Raimundo79. 22t – Milagli. 22b – Khamkhlai Thanet. 23b – creativemarc. 24 – weedezign. 25t – Robert Przybysz. 25b – Aumm graphixphoto. 26tr – Serg64. 26b – Sean Pavone. 27t – kryzhov. 27b – Chones. 28tr – Sergey Ryzhov. 28b – Alien Zagrebelnaya. 29t – faestock. 29b – Syda Productions. 30t – nikkytok. 30b – Markus Gann. Images are courtesy of Shutterstock.com. With thanks to Getty Images, Thinkstock Photo and iStockphoto.

CONTENTS

Words that look like **this** are explained in the glossary on page 31.

WHAT IS LIGHT?

Have you ever heard the expression "Let there be light"? Why do you think people say this? Think about what our lives would be like without light. Light allows us to see and enjoy the world around us.

LIGHT SOURCES

Anything that gives off light is called luminescent, as long as this light isn't given off simply because the thing is very hot. A light source that gives off light because it is very hot is said to be incandescent. The Sun is our most important source of **natural** light and without it, there would be no life on Earth. Plants, which provide food for humans and animals, need sunlight to make the energy that they need to grow. This process is called **photosynthesis**.

Plants use sunlight to change water and **carbon dioxide** into food.

Thomas Edison

Before the discovery of electricity, the only light people could use came from the Sun, fires and simple inventions like candles. At the beginning of the 1800s, several inventors produced incandescent light bulbs. However, they were not practical because they burnt out too quickly and needed batteries to work. In 1879, however, an American inventor named Thomas Edison invented the first incandescent light bulb that could be made cheaply and used easily by customers. The light bulb's **filament**, which is the part of the bulb that heats up to create light, could last for a very long time.

LIGHT ENERGY

Light is a form of energy called **electromagnetic radiation**. The centre of the Sun is being squeezed together very tightly and it is extremely hot. Because of this, the Sun gives off huge amounts of energy in the form of light and heat. Billions of other stars in the universe also give off light.

The Sun and stars are natural light sources.

VISIBLE AND INVISIBLE LIGHT

The light we can see is only a very small part of all the light in the universe. Other kinds of light include x-rays and microwaves. Even though we cannot see these kinds of light, they are still very useful to us. X-rays, for example, can pass through our bodies, but are absorbed by our bones and teeth. Because of this, we can use them to produce images that show broken bones or other problems.

X-Ray Image

HOW DOES LIGHT TRAVEL?

Light moves away from a light source in the form of waves, just like the ripples that are made on a pond if you drop in a stone. Unlike sound waves, light waves can move through a **vacuum**. This is why light can travel to Earth from the Sun through the vacuum of space. Light also moves as **particles**, called **photons**. This discovery was made by the German scientist Albert Einstein.

Albert Einstein

Light travels at almost 300,000 kilometres per second – nothing in the universe moves faster. It takes just eight minutes for light from the Sun to travel the 150 million kilometres to Earth. This means that when you see the Sun setting, it actually happened eight minutes before.

The Andromeda Galaxy is over two million **light-years** away, meaning that the light we see from it takes more than two million years to reach us.

Some luminescent things give off more light than others. The brightness of a light is known as its intensity. As you move farther away from a light source, the intensity of the light decreases. This is because the light waves spread out as they travel away from the source, just like the ripples on the pond.

Light Source

Think of the place where the stone enters the water as the light source. As they spread out, the ripples, or light waves, get weaker and weaker.

TRANSPARENT, OPAQUE AND TRANSLUCENT MATERIALS

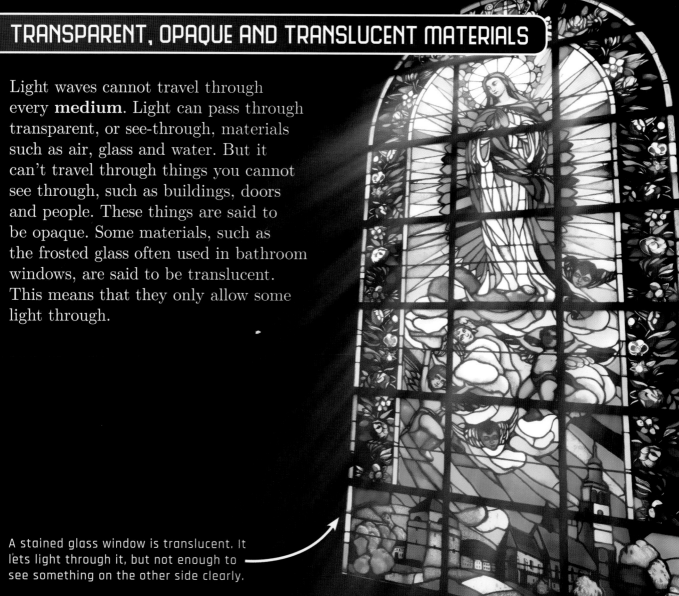

Light waves cannot travel through every **medium**. Light can pass through transparent, or see-through, materials such as air, glass and water. But it can't travel through things you cannot see through, such as buildings, doors and people. These things are said to be opaque. Some materials, such as the frosted glass often used in bathroom windows, are said to be translucent. This means that they only allow some light through.

A stained glass window is translucent. It lets light through it, but not enough to see something on the other side clearly.

SHADOWS

When light waves hit an opaque object, a dark shape, called a shadow, forms on the other side of the object.

Look carefully at the shadow cast by this tennis player. The racket's shadow is not as dark as the player's shadow because, although the strings are opaque, some light waves can pass through the gaps between the strings.

You can make shadows yourself by asking a friend to shine a torch at the wall in a dark room. Move your hands in front of the torch to create shadows on the wall. Experiment with making different shapes. You can make a bird shape by linking your thumbs together. Notice how the shadow takes on the outline of the shape you make with your hands.

In this simple shadow theatre, a light is shone onto the puppets, which casts shadows onto the screen behind them.

The next time you are outside on a sunny day, notice your shadow and how it changes as the Sun moves through the sky. In the middle of the day, when the Sun is highest in the sky, your shadow will be small. In the evening, as the Sun sinks lower in the sky, your shadow will become longer and longer. The diagram explains why this is so.

Midday Sun

Evening Sun

Small Midday Shadow

Large Evening Shadow

SOLAR ECLIPSE

As the Moon **orbits** the Earth and the Earth orbits the Sun, there are times when the Moon passes directly between the Sun and the Earth. When this happens, the Moon, which is opaque, blocks the Sun's rays from reaching the Earth and casts a shadow onto the Earth's surface. The part of the Earth that is in the Moon's shadow is plunged into darkness, even though it is daytime!

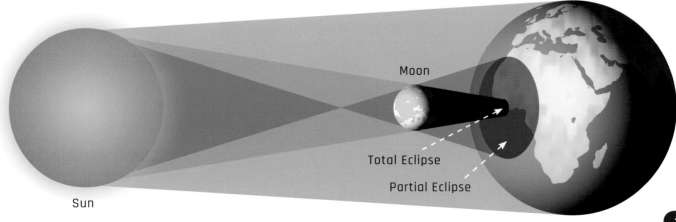

Moon

Total Eclipse

Partial Eclipse

Sun

Earth

REFLECTION, ABSORPTION AND SCATTERING

LIGHT SOURCES

If light is shone at something that it cannot pass through, some of the light will bounce back off the surface. This is known as reflection. Light rays are reflected off an object at the same angle that they hit the object, as shown below. At the same time, some of the light is absorbed. This means that it is taken in by the surface of the object, just like a sponge absorbs water.

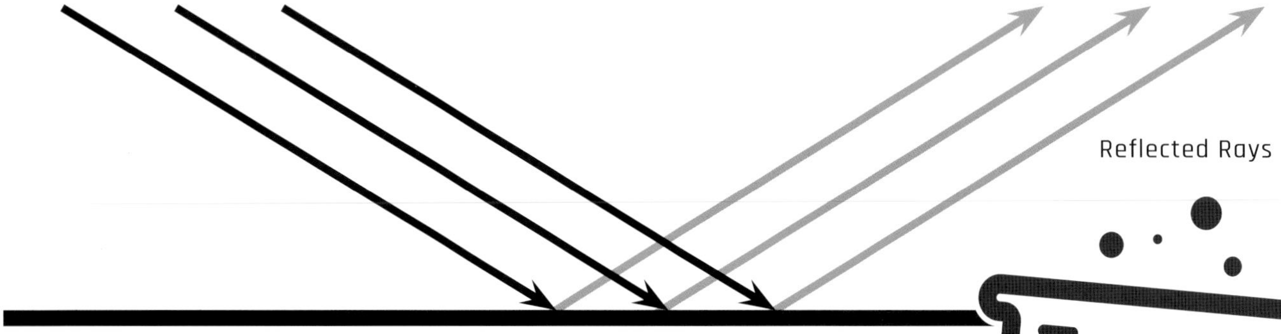

Reflected Rays

Smooth Surface

Surfaces that appear light in colour reflect more light than they absorb. Dark surfaces absorb more light than they reflect. Most objects are not a light source, meaning that they can only be seen when they reflect light from the Sun or another light source.

DID YOU KNOW? MOONLIGHT DOESN'T EXIST! WHEN THE MOON APPEARS TO BE SHINING, IT IS ACTUALLY JUST REFLECTING LIGHT FROM THE SUN

Smooth, flat, shiny surfaces are the best for reflecting light. A mirror, which is usually made from a sheet of glass with a thin layer of silver or aluminium on the back, is very reflective and reflects light in only one direction.

Lights from the bridge and surrounding buildings are reflected in the smooth surface of the River Thames in London.

You can only see your face in the mirror because light reflects off your face, bounces into the mirror and is then reflected back off the mirror and directly into your eyes. The rough surface of a brick wall reflects light waves in all directions, meaning that you cannot see your reflection in it.

Most surfaces are not completely smooth, so when light hits them, it is reflected in many different directions. This process, called scattering, enables light from the Sun to light up the Earth. When the Sun's rays hit particles in the Earth's **atmosphere**, light is scattered in all directions. It is dark in space because it is a vacuum, meaning that there are no particles to scatter the light from the Sun.

A diamond doesn't shine in the dark because it has no light source of its own. It shines in light because it is cut to reflect light in many different directions, which makes it sparkle.

REFRACTION

Rather than reflecting or absorbing light, transparent materials, such as water and air, allow light to pass through them. When light waves move from one substance (such as air) into another substance with a different density (such as water), they change speed and appear to bend. This bending is called refraction. Light waves speed up when they move into a less dense substance and slow down when they move into a more dense substance.

Straws in water look bent because light rays are refracted as they move from the more dense water to the less dense air.

THE DENSITY OF SOMETHING DESCRIBES HOW CLOSELY ITS PARTICLES ARE PACKED TOGETHER.

Archer fish feed on insects. They knock them out of the air and into the water by firing a jet of water from their mouths. Because the fish are in the water and the insects are in the air, they have had to learn to adjust their aim to account for light refraction!

Mirages play tricks on our eyes and make us see things that are not really there. Desert mirages occur because light is refracted as it travels through patches of air with different densities.

DIFFRACTION

When light waves pass through small openings or near to the edges of opaque objects, they can spread out in all directions. This is called diffraction and it is similar, in effect, to putting your thumb over the end of a hosepipe to make the water spray out in all directions.

When light rays are diffracted, it causes a rainbow-like effect called iridescence. You can see this effect on the surface of a soap bubble or on the shiny side of a CD. This effect is very different from rainbows you see in the sky, which are not caused by iridescence.

There are tiny bumps on the shiny surfaces of CDs. When light waves enter the spaces between these bumps, the light is diffracted. This causes the iridescence that you see when you tilt the disk.

COLOURS

Visible light is the light that we can see. It seems to be colourless and is also known as white light. It is actually made up of seven different colours of light; red, orange, yellow, green, blue, indigo and violet. Together they make up the visible light spectrum. 'Spectrum' means a band or range.

In 1666, a scientist called Sir Isaac Newton discovered that white light could be split into different colours. He shone a beam of sunlight through a wedge of glass called a prism. The prism refracted the light and split it into its separate colours. The process of splitting light is called dispersion.

Sir Isaac Newton

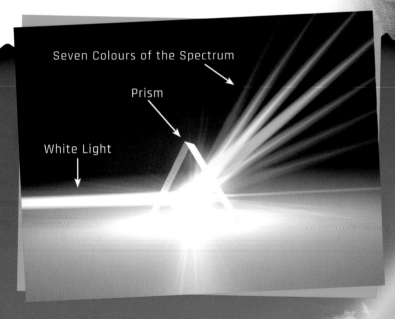

Seven Colours of the Spectrum

Prism

White Light

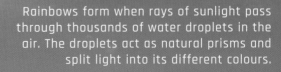

Rainbows form when rays of sunlight pass through thousands of water droplets in the air. The droplets act as natural prisms and split light into its different colours.

SEEING COLOURS

All paints and coloured objects contain pigments. Pigments are substances that absorb some of the colours in light and reflect others. We see an object as being a particular colour because the object reflects only light of that colour, absorbing all the other colours in the spectrum.

We see grass as green because it reflects green light and absorbs all the other colours in the light spectrum.

DID YOU KNOW? LIGHT FROM THE SUN IS SCATTERED BY TINY PARTICLES IN THE ATMOSPHERE. BLUE LIGHT IS SCATTERED MORE THAN ANY OTHER COLOUR OF LIGHT BECAUSE IT TRAVELS IN VERY SHORT WAVES. THAT'S WHY THE SKY APPEARS BLUE!

This penguin's white feathers reflect all colours of light. Its black feathers absorb all colours of light.

MIXING COLOURS

Almost any colour can be made by mixing different amounts of the primary colours of light – red, green and blue. When two primary colours are mixed, they make the secondary colours – cyan, magenta and yellow.

Red

Yellow

Green

White

Magenta

Cyan

Blue

VISION

HOW DO WE SEE?

We can only see things when light reflects off objects and enters our eyes through our pupils. The pupil is the small opening at the front of the eye that appears black. The iris, which is the coloured part of the eye, is a ring of muscle around the pupil. It controls how much light enters the eye by changing the size of the pupil.

The pupil is covered by the cornea, which is the clear, outer part of the eye. As light rays pass through the pupil, they enter the lens, which is a jelly-like disc. The shape of the lens can be changed by the muscles around it. Both the cornea and the lens refract the light rays entering the eye so that they are directed onto the retina, which is the tissue at the back of the eye.

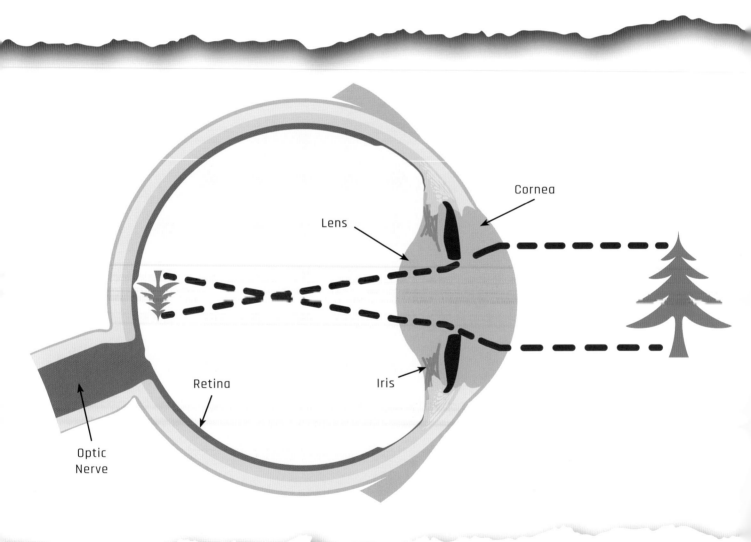

Cornea

Lens

Retina

Iris

Optic Nerve

IT'S AN UPSIDE DOWN WORLD

The retina is a thin layer of **cells** at the back of the eye that reacts to light. These cells send messages along the **optic nerve** to the brain. The image – made up of different coloured lights – that is projected on the retina is actually upside down. However, our brain instantly flips the image the right way up so that we can make sense of what we are seeing. The retina is called a photoreceptor, which means that it reacts to light.

Retina cells are made up of two types of photoreceptor, called rods and cones. Rods allow you to work out light from dark and they help you to see in dim light. Cones are sensitive to different colours and help you to see in bright light. They allow you to see the difference between colours and between different shades of the same colour.

DID YOU KNOW? ABOUT HALF OF THE HUMAN BRAIN IS DEDICATED TO SIGHT.

ANIMAL VISION

Some animals' eyes work differently from our eyes. The eyes of many insects, such as flies and bees, contain many tiny lenses instead of just one. Each lens projects a piece of an image into the eye and the insect's brain then puts all the pieces together like a puzzle to make one single image.

Have you ever heard someone described as 'eagle-eyed' because they have good eyesight? This is because eagles and vultures actually have far better vision than humans. Their retinas have about five times the number of rods and cones than ours have. This helps them to see mice and other **prey** from a great height in the sky – over three kilometres away.

Horseflies have very large eyes so that as much light as possible can enter them.

Golden Eagle

17

LENSES AND VISION PROBLEMS

The word 'lens' can refer to any piece of transparent material that has a curved surface and refracts light that passes through it. Because of this, both the jelly-like disc in your eye and the glass in a pair of spectacles are known as lenses. There are two main types of lens – convex and concave. Convex lenses have surfaces that curve outwards and concave lenses have surfaces that curve inwards.

Convex Lens   Concave Lens

USING LENSES

Convex and concave lenses are found in many useful pieces of equipment. Cameras use lenses to focus the light reflected off both near and distant objects, making it so that both appear clearly in a photograph. Lenses are also used in microscopes, helping scientists to study things that are too small to see with the naked eye, and in telescopes, which allow people to get a close-up look at stars and planets.

Lenses can bend light to make things look bigger. This is called magnification. The lenses in microscopes help scientists to see things that they would not be able to see normally, like these E. coli bacteria, which cause food poisoning.

SHORT AND LONG SIGHT

The lenses in the eyes change shape in order to **focus** light from both near and distant objects onto the retina. However, some people's lenses do not work properly. Short-sighted people can see near objects clearly, but find that distant objects appear fuzzy. Their lenses focus the picture of what they are seeing just in front of the retina. Long-sighted people can see distant objects clearly, but find that near objects appear fuzzy. Their lenses focus the picture just behind the retina. The lenses in spectacles or contact lenses refract light before it enters the eye so that it is focussed perfectly onto the retina. This helps the wearer to see both near and far objects clearly again.

Short Sight

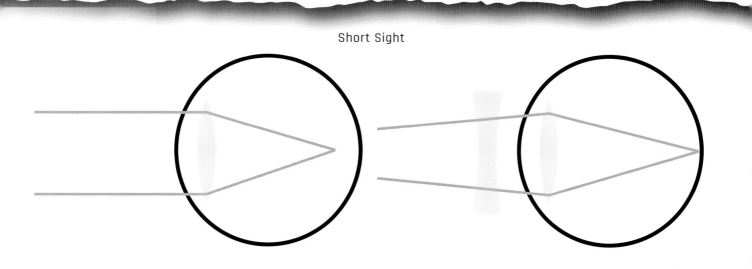

Concave lenses help short-sighted people to see distant objects clearly.

Long Sight

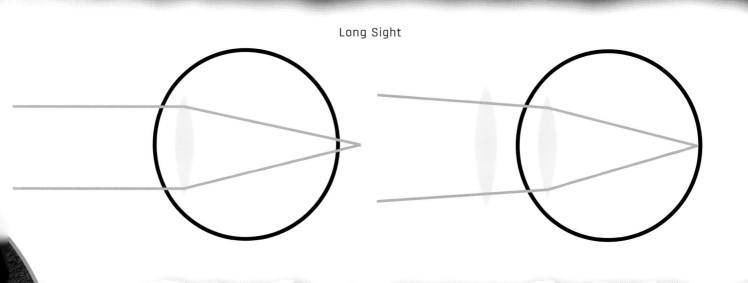

Convex lenses help long-sighted people to see near objects clearly.

CAMERAS

Cameras use lenses to focus light onto film or a **sensor**. The film or sensor then records the image, meaning we can view the picture again and again. The earliest cameras stored images on sheets of metal or glass. These sheets were coated with substances that were sensitive to light. Today, some cameras store pictures on a light-sensitive film, which can be used to print photographs. Digital cameras store pictures electronically.

A special curved camera lens, called a fisheye lens, can be used to create unusual, circular images.

DIGITAL CAMERAS

Digital cameras were invented in the 1990s. They record pictures onto special, light-sensitive equipment. Images recorded by digital cameras are broken down into tiny coloured squares called pixels. Information about the pixels is stored in the camera's memory. A **microchip** in the camera pieces together the pixels to make an image we can print out or see on a computer screen.

The amount of detail in an image is known as its resolution. The greater the number of pixels, the higher the resolution will be. This high resolution picture shows these cherries in amazing detail.

20

NIGHT VISION

Night vision goggles and cameras help us to see and record images even when in darkness. As we have seen, our vision and cameras depend on visible light. As darkness is the lack of visible light, night vision goggles and cameras have to use a different process to allow us to see and record images. Night vision equipment gathers a type of light that we cannot see – infrared light. Special equipment then changes the infrared light into green light so that we can see it. They use green light because the human eye can detect more shades of green than of any other colour.

Night vision goggles help the wearer to see clearly in the dark. They are often worn by soldiers who need to move about or attack a target at night.

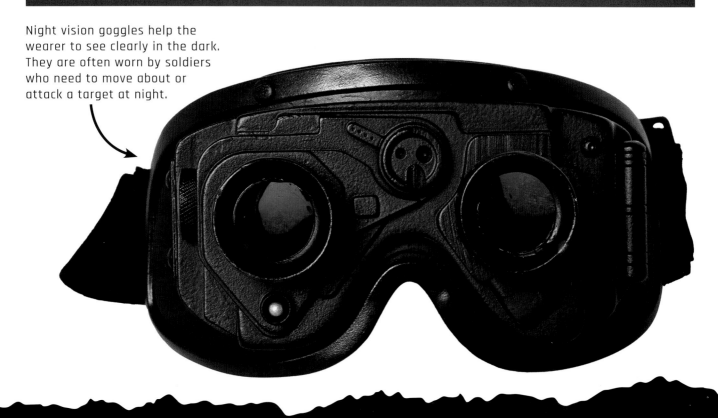

Night vision cameras allow wildlife films to include shots of animals at night, such as this image of a giraffe.

THE LIGHT SPECTRUM

Electromagnetic Spectrum

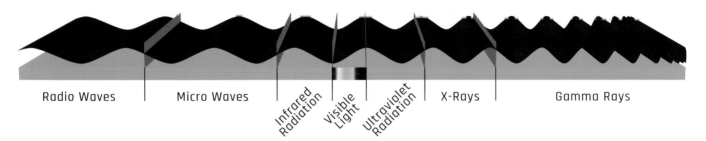

Radio Waves | Micro Waves | Infrared Radiation | Visible Light | Ultraviolet Radiation | X-Rays | Gamma Rays

As the diagram shows, the light we can see is only a very small portion of all the light that exists. Light we cannot see with our eyes alone is said to be in the invisible light spectrum. Scientists have worked out many ways to detect and use these invisible lights.

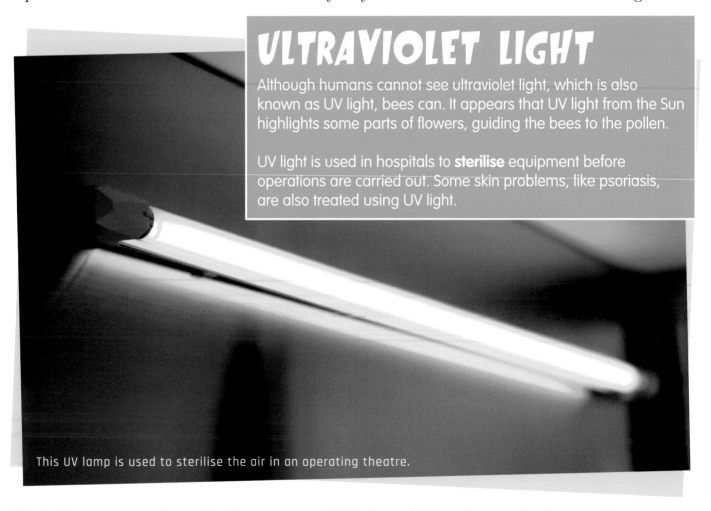

ULTRAVIOLET LIGHT

Although humans cannot see ultraviolet light, which is also known as UV light, bees can. It appears that UV light from the Sun highlights some parts of flowers, guiding the bees to the pollen.

UV light is used in hospitals to **sterilise** equipment before operations are carried out. Some skin problems, like psoriasis, are also treated using UV light.

This UV lamp is used to sterilise the air in an operating theatre.

The light we receive from the Sun contains UV light, which makes our bodies produce vitamin D. We need vitamin D for strong teeth and bones. However, too much exposure to UV light can be harmful for us. It can cause sunburn and may eventually lead to skin **cancer**.

GAMMA RAYS

Gamma rays are another type of invisible light. They are given off by **radioactive** materials, for example uranium. Uranium is a substance used to produce electricity in nuclear **power station**s. Gamma rays are also given off from naturally radioactive substances around us in the air and soil.

USING GAMMA RAYS

In hospitals, high doses of gamma rays can be used to destroy cancer cells. Gamma rays are also used by companies that make food. They are used to kill any **bacteria** that might be in food. This process is called irradiation.

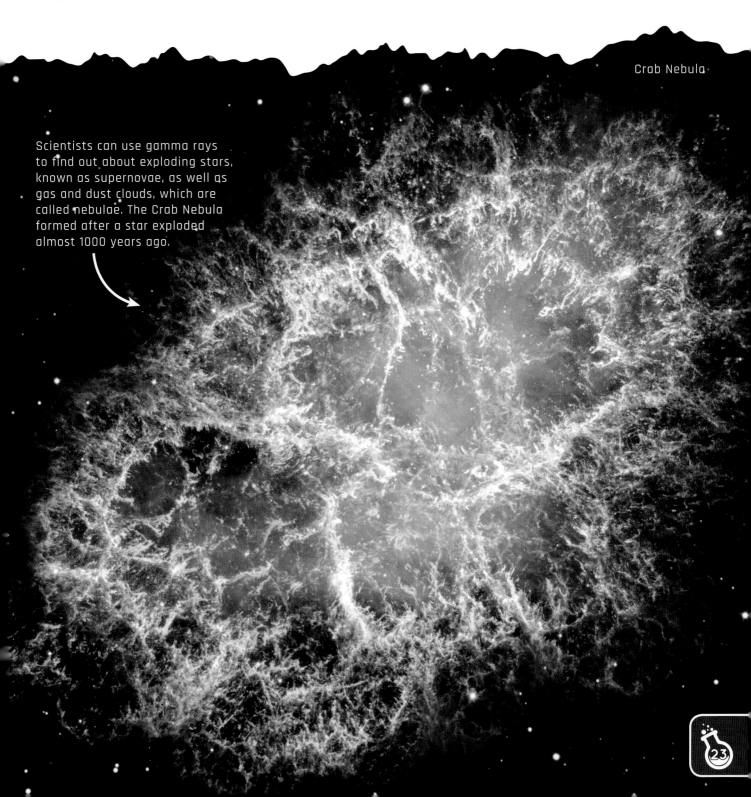

Crab Nebula

Scientists can use gamma rays to find out about exploding stars, known as supernovae, as well as gas and dust clouds, which are called nebulae. The Crab Nebula formed after a star exploded almost 1000 years ago.

LASERS

Laser light is a special form of light created by a laser machine. As we have seen, white light is made up of the different colours of the visible spectrum. Each colour has its own **wavelength** and **frequency**. Laser light, however, is made up of only one wavelength of light. It is also made of only one frequency – or colour – of light.

Unlike white light waves, which spread out in all directions, laser light waves travel **parallel** to one another and do not scatter, even over long distances. This makes laser beams very narrow and means that they can be focussed onto one spot. This makes them very useful.

Many music concerts include laser light shows.

DID YOU KNOW?
AS LASER LIGHT IS MADE UP OF JUST ONE WAVELENGTH, IT CANNOT BE SEPARATED BY A PRISM. THE WAVES ALL TRAVEL AT THE SAME SPEED THROUGH THE PRISM.

Each laser beam is made up of parallel waves of laser light.

USING LASER LIGHT

Lasers have many uses in hospitals. Surgeons sometimes use lasers instead of **scalpels** because they cut skin very neatly. This helps wounds to heal quickly without forming scars. Lasers can also be used to seal wounds without the need for stitches.

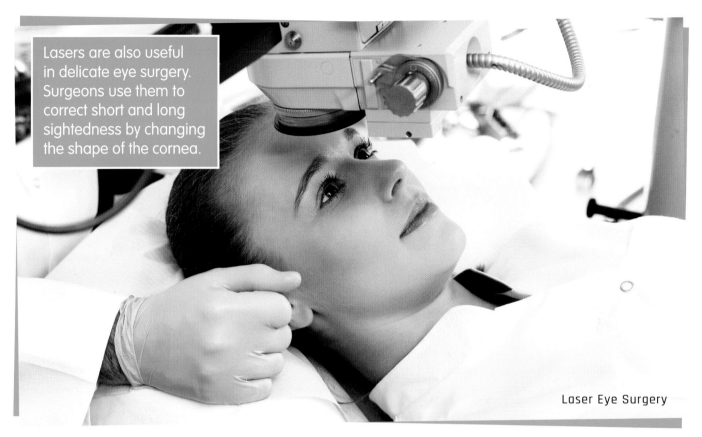

Lasers are also useful in delicate eye surgery. Surgeons use them to correct short and long sightedness by changing the shape of the cornea.

Laser Eye Surgery

Lasers are powerful enough to cut through tough materials like metals and even diamonds. In clothing factories, they are used to cut through hundreds of layers of fabric at a time, saving time and money.

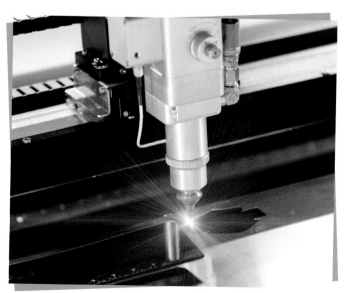

This laser is being used to cut through a metal sheet.

American astronauts Buzz Aldrin and Neil Armstrong left mirrors on the Moon after their moonwalk in 1969. The mirrors can reflect laser beams sent from Earth. Scientists have timed how long it takes for lasers to reach the Moon, bounce off the mirrors and return to Earth. From this, they were able to work out the exact distance between the Earth and the Moon. They also worked out that the Moon is moving away from the Earth by about 3.8 centimetres every year.

LIGHTBULBS AND LEDS

Old-fashioned light bulbs like this are incandescent. This means that they give off light because they are very hot.

To make light bulbs give off light, electricity is sent through a thin coiled wire, called the filament, which heats up and glows. If you have ever accidentally touched one of these bulbs while it is on, you will know they can get very hot! This is because, most of the electricity - around 95% of it - is wasted as heat rather than light. These bulbs have now been largely replaced by lamps that use much less energy by converting much more of the electrical energy into light.

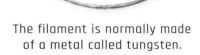

Filament

The filament is normally made of a metal called tungsten.

NEON LIGHTS

Many of the brightly coloured lights seen on buildings at night are **neon** lights.

Neon lights are said to be luminescent, which means they give off light but not heat. These bulbs are filled with neon gas, which glows a reddish orange colour when electricity is passed through it. Adding other substances to neon produces different colours. For example, adding **mercury** to the neon gives off blue light.

Compact Fluorescent Lamps, or CFLs, were the first type of energy-saving lamps. 'Compact' means small.

Regular fluorescent lamps contain a gas that gives off UV light when electricity is passed through it. This UV light makes substances inside the fluorescent lamps, called phosphors, give off a light that we can see. CFLs use far less energy than these old-fashioned bulbs. Almost all the electricity they use is turned into light energy and they give off very little heat. They are, therefore, much cheaper to run than incandescent bulbs.

Compact
Fluorescent
Lamp

CFLs are now being replaced by LED – Light-Emitting Diode – bulbs like these. If something is said to be 'light-emitting', it means that it gives off light. A diode is something that allows electricity to pass through it.

LEDs last longer and use even less energy than CFLs. They reach their maximum brightness straightaway and don't need time to warm up. They are also easier to **recycle** than CFLs.

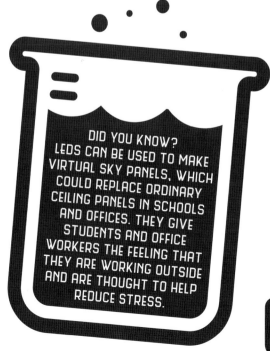

DID YOU KNOW?
LEDS CAN BE USED TO MAKE VIRTUAL SKY PANELS, WHICH COULD REPLACE ORDINARY CEILING PANELS IN SCHOOLS AND OFFICES. THEY GIVE STUDENTS AND OFFICE WORKERS THE FEELING THAT THEY ARE WORKING OUTSIDE AND ARE THOUGHT TO HELP REDUCE STRESS.

Have a look round your house and see what types of bulb you can find. Be careful not to touch the bulbs, in case they are very hot.

LIGHT IN THE FUTURE

CONTACT LENSES

The idea of contact lenses was first put forward in 1508 by the famous Italian painter and inventor Leonardo da Vinci. The first wearable lenses were made from glass in 1888 by a Swiss doctor, Adolf Fick. They covered the whole surface of the eye and would have been uncomfortable to wear.

Modern lenses are made from thin, soft plastic and are comfortable to wear.

Scientists are currently trying to perfect a spray-on contact lens. The spray would contain a special substance that matched the **prescription** of the wearer and would dry on to the surface of the eyeball. The substance would then refract light onto the retina. These spray-on lenses are being designed to wear off after 24 hours. Different coloured lenses could also be used for fancy dress or by actors in films.

NOW YOU SEE ME ...

Scientists are developing a special ultra-thin material that changes the normal flow of light waves. Light waves that hit an object covered in this material would be directed around it, being neither reflected nor absorbed. The object would, therefore, appear to be invisible. This idea is still being developed and only works on very small objects at the moment, but one day, you could have your very own invisibility cloak!

HOLOGRAMS

A hologram is like a three dimensional photograph that is created using laser light. You can see simple holograms on paper money and credit cards. They are used to stop criminals from copying these items.

Scientists are also working on a process that creates holograms of patients' **organs**. These holograms would give doctors more detailed information than scans can provide.

These pupils are studying a hologram of the globe. Ordinary photographs are 2D, meaning they are flat images. Holograms are **3D**.

EXPERIMENTS WITH LIGHT

MAKE A RAINBOW SPINNER

You can see the colours of the visible spectrum come together to make white light by making a rainbow spinner.

1 First, make a neat circle on cardboard using a compass or by drawing round a jar.

2 Carefully cut it out.

3 Next, divide the circle into seven equal sections and paint them the seven colours of the rainbow.

4 Push a pencil through the middle and spin it on the floor or on a table.

5 As it spins, the different coloured light reflecting off it will mix together to form white light.

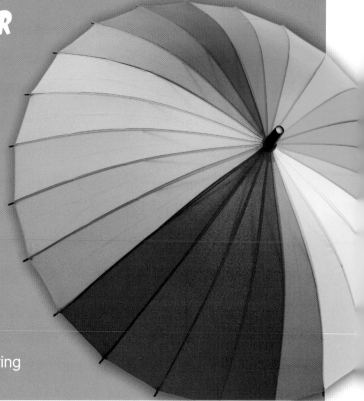

Spinning this rainbow umbrella would create white light.

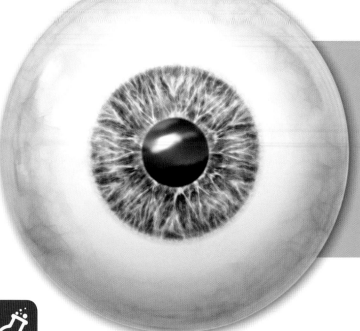

PUPIL POWER

Sit in a darkened room, then put the light on and look in a mirror straightaway. You should notice that your pupils are very large. In dimly lit rooms, the pupil opens up to let more light into the eye in order to help you see better. Now shine a bright torch near, but not directly in, your eyes. What do you notice about your pupils when you look in the mirror now? Why is this?

GLOSSARY

3D	an object which has height, width and depth
atmosphere	the layer of gases surrounding the Earth
bacteria	tiny organisms that can cause infection
cancer	a serious illness that makes the body produce more cells than it should
carbon dioxide	a gas that occurs naturally in the atmosphere
cells	the individual units from which all animals and plants are made
electromagnetic radiation	the spectrum of light energy that stars release into space and which moves through space in the form of waves and particles
filament	the metal wire in a lightbulb that glows when electricity is passed through it
focus	make light waves come together at a single point
frequency	the number of waves that pass any given point in a second
light-years	units of distance equivalent to the distance that light travels in one year (9.46 trillion kilometres)
medium	a substance through which waves can travel
mercury	a silvery-white liquid metal
microchip	a tiny piece of electronic equipment that can hold large amounts of information
natural	not made by humans
neon	a gas that glows when electricity is passed through it
optic nerve	a bundle of fine threads that send information about what we are seeing from the eye to the brain
orbits	travels around a larger object in a roughly circular path
organs	parts of an organism that have an important job or function
parallel	side by side, with a constant distance between
particles	extremely small pieces of a substance
photons	particles of light energy
photosynthesis	a process in which plants use sunlight to make food
power stations	places where electricity is produced
prescription	information about the type of lens needed to correct someone's sight
prey	animals that are hunted by other animals for food
radioactive	giving off radiation, which is a harmful form of energy
recycle	use again or to make something else
scalpels	small, sharp knives used by surgeons
sensor	a device that detects – or picks up – light waves
sterilise	clean thoroughly to remove harmful bacteria
vacuum	a space from which all particles of matter, including air, have been removed
wavelength	the distance between the same point on any two waves

INDEX